To those who long for something
they cannot quite reach unless it is in
turning pages like rustling leaves by a
quiet brook.

Contents

ART OF BLINDLY BELIEVING

Just when daisies bloomed
And in the spring, little elves groomed
The spring thunderstorm,
It struck the homes
Of the hares and gnomes.
In the moonlight they claim
It gets better no matter the blame
But oh! Little do they know
The roots of venom
The bigger they grow.
Hope shines through
As the ray of sunlight grew
But a small part of every being
Now fears the art
Of blindly believing.

Everything About Love:

Love is a beautiful thing
It flows through all realities
It blooms far and wide, with no conditions.
Free from destiny, it spreads its vigor like ivies.
Love slows us down.
Love makes us want to be there for each other.
Like a garden of evening primroses and peonies, swaying.
Love is in the air.
When warmth and love spreads inside the cocoon shell,
Love makes us want to do grand things.
From the purr of a cat to the warmth of a hug,
It emphasizes the silly innocence of loving eternally.
There's always something and someone to love
For I compare thee to a ravishing spring day.
Like the righteous sunshine caressing the meadows in May.
You spread your love like the lily of the valley.
Fly high, like the lark ascending with all its might
Bloom wide, like hydrangeas in the very daylight.
I stand anew in my world of allure
As I hold you the mirror for my cure.

Wither Away

Just as the leaves fall in the autumn
Just as the raindrops pour from the sky
Like the stones at the bank erode away
So does my hope for you wither away

Error 403 — Forbidden

Last night got me thinking of you.
You aren't going to stay, are you?
(Stay. A while longer today.)
Only if you feel like it, isn't it?
Fortune is a fickle friend, they say
And I'm tired of chasing fate
When I look into your bashful eyes,
I know you feel the same.
How does it feel to share your world with me?
I would never know.
Loving you from a distance
Is how I understand you. And feel you.
Funny how spring never came again
Since the day you slipped away in the dead of night
On a frozen Friday
When you were my sun, my only source of warmth.
How does it feel to be on the receiving end?
I would never know.
I envy your friends and loved ones
For they have you all for themselves- your love is theirs.
Let me be a part of your world.
Maybe the broken pieces of my heart
Could keep you company
As long as you're asleep, sound, and fine.
How does it feel to caress your gentle face?
I will never know.
To look at you as you fall asleep
And to hold your hands in the cold.
Does it ever occur to you?
That the stars, the sunset, the trees
And the little sweet boxes
Remind me of you?
Over the horizon, when the sun wakes up
I believe there's nothing for me here.
I'm trying hard to break from this routine
Of keeping you. Next to me. Nonchalantly.

Who am I to you?
Am I just a mere entertainer to you?
Late realizations will be the death of me
But remember just tell me the truth.
Remind me why I choose you every day
Please and cry for you every day.
Let me hear the grass grow
And your heartbeat echoing in my anxious, ebbing ears
Listen to me, no, I should be listening to you
Trust me, I only want to hear you speak
But I'm just another girl on the wire
Bleeding for you. I'm not yours.
Before it's too late, tell me one last time
That you'll see me on the other side
And that you'll hold me close
Like how you do, to yourself.
Tell me you'll take care of yourselves
Tell me you'll remember that you're always a good human
Tell me that these reminders were not a joke to you,
No, I don't want to know.
The only world I can ever see is you
And I don't think I could run out of love for you
Or maybe I am, I can't tell
I'm tired of fighting the fight.

You're not mine to keep,
You're everybody else's.
And everybody else is yours
I'm just the fool you've made of.
I hope she takes good care of you.
I hope she writes your poems of love
When you lay in her arms
As the moonlight tests the night
In the faintest of lights
When my pillow weeps,
Make sure to stay bright and
Be the one and only.

Heart as a wildflower

Hearts are believed to be fragile
But little do they know
It is the strongest thing to ever exist
Rebuilding itself even after being trampled
Being burnt, and tossed out without a care
It survives everything
Like a wildflower.

Endless Tides:

In the vast, ceaseless churning of the oceans
With the ethereal whispers of the wind to keep me company,
I await my awakening like the whale song that sails toward new horizons,
In the morning tide as the oceans rise.
As I long for the sea to swallow me,
With the gentle waves lapping subtly on the shore,
I see my endless slumber so free without you.
With the lodestar keeping me safe, like a warm embrace.
And I try to rise like Amphitrite with all my might
Even as the strength in my scars stays an unknown outcome,
Let me rest awhile in the serene seas,
Please be my abyss of freedom, boundless sea.
The frigid days were calling out to me
Reminding me how our days are numbered and wired.
As the tranquil tides danced perilously,
I remind the ocean to knock me down.
Swallow me, sea, into the vast horizons of emptiness
I am no one.
Or better,
I am not yours.

Wonder

Your eyes they light up like celestial stars
Your smile giving off that October
comfort
Just the way you are never fails to make
me wonder
How I ever thought that there was
someone better.

Through the Night:

Where dawn and dusk are interwoven in this full blue twilight
I unfurl gently as the queen of the night.
Butterflies rain in this blossoming garden you've built
As we venture into the unknown beyond dawn's embrace
Silence falls in the way of shyness in our bashful eyes
While I turn into a blue sky making the winds embrace
The swaying blossom tree by the moonlit river
Where the tender leaves fall on the weeping rock as an embrace.
Beneath the canopy of trees where the winds caress
Us like the slow waltz of your heartbeat
As I sink into his fragrance in the fresh rain
And the whirlpool of this intoxicating moment of fervor.
The night hums a lullaby only we hear
As we tread through the stillness under the moon's watchful eyes.
Lost in the twilight where time stands still as I melt into you,
I feel eternity, a hastening urge, never to let you go.
For every melody you sing, I'll breathe a verse
For every dawn you greet, I'll wish upon every star
To stay in the solace of your eternal grace
While the moon casts her shadows on our intertwined hearts.

Autumn

The leaves like confetti dances in the breeze
Falling gracefully from the trees
Rain threatening to pour
The moon casting its glow

The smell of cinnamon wafting
The fiery orange sun casting
Its warm rays on the ground
And the feeling of peace found

There's a sense of peace in a way
In waking up everyday
The season of autumn giving comfort
The sense of belonging rediscovered.

Ephemerality

Atop the wildflower hills, I await my dirge
Through the heavy mist, the symbol of disdain emerges
Under this duress, I clash with a virge
In the uncanny night of this mundane world's purge

The candlelight burned eternally,
While the sunshine's blues sang like an elegy
It's time to step out, jovially
To emphasize, not discount, the innocent silliness of loving, tirelessly.
The Adenium blooms where the path unfurls
For pride is the mask of our sins
The enlivening moon rises, leaving me asking
Will it shine over me or you, masking?

Home

A beautiful laugh from the soul
A smile lighting up the town
The puzzle pieces who make me whole
And turn a frown upside down

A feeling of tranquility
And that of peace
Only to be found in the city
Deep within the heart crease

Each eyes shine like home
Each hug, A comfort like no other
A void on my own
Which only they could fill like no other

Maybe nothing else can replicate it
But this forever in my heart it will sit.

Eternal Living Proof:

This wildflower love is eternal for life.
As you flow like the mountain of strength,
Do I hold on to you forever in this labyrinth?
Or do I let you bloom like the hyacinth?
Your endless embrace, want your ever-loving grace
Growing like ivies climbing over as solace
And as I look at you so merrily
You spread your vigor, like the lily of the valley
As the moon rests through the sorrow of the night
And as jasmines and gladioli unfurl under the moonlight
I long for my Aphrodite woven in saffron callas.
As I yearn for you, the Northern star, of my starry atlas.
Where dawn and dusk weave our tale in the twilight,
Echoes of our love ring like yesternight.
Be the living proof of my story,
Be the light that God has given.

Rain

In a sky of gray, a misty veil
Raindrops tell a fairy tale.
With different hues,
And a garden of muse,
With soft refrain,
The song of rain.

Blue:

It was time to go home —
To the place my soul belongs.
Alone, with the thought of you
Killing me softly with an unbearable lightness.
As I waited quietly in the airport,
I watched people that reminded me of your warmth
Cheerful smiles on the daughter that quietly nudged her mother of her youth
And the quiet intimacy of locking eyes with a stranger made me think of you.
The lone man underneath the tent miles away from home
Looked out for people who travel miles away to their homes
Maybe they too didn't belong, in a place called home
When they struggle to fit in from one place to another.
The azure had me fooled by its limits
With the skies below me and the waterfalls that look like cobwebs
I wonder how it feels to smell the clouds that surround me
And to stay afloat for a day, without you on my mind.
We're all invisible from above
Yet there will be ones to humble you
Pay no heed, for they destroy their own lives
With judgments, stares, and acts that idle people do.
Maybe these are your reminders
To keep you in light during my bluest days.
I'm home again.
But not blue for you'll never be my home.

Live by you

Maybe in the pure golden light of the sun
Or under the silver drape of the moon
Hope you find a reason to
Live by the truest version of you.

Sakura, Sakura

Blossom by blossom the spring begins
Sakura, sakura where have you been?

Gentle and subtle like its origins
Softly flowing, soaring in the air.

Over the hills and the fields
High up in the vernal winds,

The redolent blossoms have passed me by
A tale of hope and renewal begins thereby

It passes a moonlit river with spring flowers at night
Till then, I carry on a blossoming spring with delight.

Stories unfold

Paged whispers turn, a stolen glance,
Coffee steam curls, a shared expanse.
Words ignite, a spark takes hold,
Hearts turn chapters, stories unfold.
Cups clink soft, a silent vow,
Lost in worlds, yet truly found
Love's sweet aroma fills us now.

Good at Imagining:

You say your name means "God has given"
But maybe even Satan himself traded you with God, the pity.
Your lackluster performance in life's theatrics
Has not yet gotten you accolades, I wonder why.

Don't forget, this is just imagination. Thank God.
Reminiscing the days and nights I've worried over you,
I find myself dancing like a clown at the crossroads of life
When all you did was pull my strings and dance along.

Maybe marrying you would be a wild thing to even think of.
Waking up to dreadful mornings while you quietly sit aside
Drinking that 'perfect' coffee you've made tasting of cardboard.
As you prance about like a toy from a metal factory, in my mind.

Don't forget, this is just imagination. Thank God.
I should be praying from the gutters with all due silence
For deafening me with your dismissiveness.
Oh, forgive me—you're the God, after all!

My imagination runs wild, as you say, for I "have no limits"
Yes, I thought about you breaking me- in body and mind.
For respect is a word long forgotten in your lustful, arrogant eyes.
As you live by the definition of a rogue in flesh

Don't forget, this is just imagination. Thank God.
I should be following you like a martyr
My thoughts dismissed, my worth reduced— you call it entitlement.
Oh, forgive me—I almost forgot. I'm the clown in your circus.

Fatherless actions and words are how you thrive
With inflated ego and pride that reeks of dead meat.
Maybe you should consider eating your fat, black heart.
Rise and shine, you bastard, no one can hear you.

A whole soul

The calm in the roaring storm
A meadow of solitude to call my own
a feeling of comfort warm
a switch of home unbeknown

no cups of coffee could ever compare
to the love I receive and care
makes me feel like I'm the center of the
universe
and nothing could ever shine more luminous.

My heart unravels every time I get a glimpse
the whole soul with all its quips.

Dial Tones:

I'd rather talk to a wall than talk to you
To tell the truth, I'll confide myself in strangers anew.
Lost in the heat of the dying fire, I'm left unheard.
By your ignorance and "space".
Even though I'm just another girl on the wire
Dancing to your dial tones like a fool loving you
For the deflection you've mastered, I stand shameless
Drooling over every insincere compliment you make,
Say something please, don't let me go
In the capricious chase for your warmth, I yearn for your presence.
Grant me this indulgence,
You'll always be a part of my soul.
Am I a threat to you?
Step
By
Step
You
Push
Me
Maybe I can't tell what's reverie or what's reality.
Oh wait, I'm overthinking again, isn't it?

The number you've called is currently unavailable.

Call ended.

LOVE IS HOME

Just between us, tell me
Oh! What is love to you?
Is it like a sweet nectarine?
Or is it a thorn filled rose?

I reckon its different for everybody
One person basking in it
While another broken down
And battered due to its viciousness

I guess we can say that
Love is home,
The sense of belonging
And the feeling of comfort.

Tsöliin nar jargakh:

The dawn storm blows
Clouding everything in sight
But the sunlight overshadows
The beautiful, chromatic Gobi Desert
Gazing across the desert,
That runs miles and miles
I wonder what I could find
In the unfathomable expanse of drylands
And as the dune unfurls
And as the sun rests and dwindles
I hear the galloping sounds of horses
Just when I thought I was losing track of time
And then I see a dusty waltz
Silhouettes of dreams on shifting times
A tsöliin nar jargakh, the desert sunset
That showed me heaven to the ground

False Poet

So much to say yet no words flow
Writing it all but feeling it's a no show
Maybe you think it is not good enough
But unable to keep it in your sleeve cuff
Writing it all to relate,
Or writing it all, yet private
Does not make you a false poet.

Adjusting

You and I are meant to be,
Like Eros and Psyche—
You wiped my cloud of sleep away,
And saw the best in me every day.
You took me from wastelands to highways,
Taught me to know my worth always.
I saw the light, you lifted me high,
Unlocking my heart from life's closed ties.
You flew, like a butterfly,
But held your ground, despite the strife.
Loving you was everything—
Did you love me the same? I wonder still.
For our love affair taught us what's free,
What's true, wise, and honest to see.
But now you've gone, and left me grieving—
A tale that ends in quiet tragedy.
Our hearts said goodbye,
Yet loving you
Feels eternal—
Or does it?
So I flourished, like the Edelweiss,
But I long for what we left behind.
In the land where camellias bloom,
Won't you come and meet me soon?
Bluebells flow gently
And the ivy grows wild—
Do I cling to the past,
Or learn to reconcile?

Not just a part of me

A little bit of this and a little bit of that
A whole world in our hands
No matter where you go, I will be a shadow
Because staying alone is not worth the sorrow.
I would give you the whole world if it meant saving your tears,
Losing you might just be my biggest fear.
I know it is not easy being an overthinker,
But I hope, my love and respect is enough for you to linger.
I am not the one to give you a part of me,
But in fact my entire mind and soul is yours, to see.
So my love, i wonder how much longer to wait,
Until i can be with you when the day ends.
And hold you when you are tired,
Making your troubles integrate and scattered.

You

Walking down the drab, grey streets
Two lovers in the night, red and white
Hold each other in the moonlight's quiet test
While I lay, weeping on my couch, falling asleep in the 'eternal rest'.
For every touch you give, I'll craft a prayer.
In the wake of losing you, I find myself buried
Under the noise of empty promises you made
Only to find myself living in a daze not to fall behind.
By the brightest corner of the quiet library
Grew the wisterias that I bought for you last week
In the hopes of seeing you for eternity.
Maybe eternity is also a joke, I'm unsure.
As the mountains lay open, bare
To the clouds that reach out and caress her like a lover
Whispering secrets only the earth can hold.
I wonder if it reminds you that's what I've wished and cried for too.
The same sun comes up and goes down every day.
Its light still lingers to heal the shadows where your memory hides.
But with each rotation, the world becomes smaller.
As if time too wishes to forget your dreary name.
So I sit, waiting in the stillness you've bought-
The wisterias were left to fade for their dismal demise.
And as the sun rises again, I am still here,
Buried beneath the weight of the world and the echoes of us that
never were.

Lost in the crowd

A cold spirit, drifting about
A crackling fire but no warmth is let out.
Maybe it can go huddle with the others
But are there no cracks for it to slip under?

It just knows that maybe somewhere it will fit in
But how much longer until the cold fully sets in
Surrounded by noise but its own not heard
Deeply embracing itself, a hope deferred.

Begging for an understanding, an embrace to warm up its inside
But when is that going to be a fulfilled desire?
But it is the hope that keeps it going that one day
The warmth that others give right now,
Will be its own to give, Through its own kin

An Eclipsed Elegy

Atop the wildflower hills, I await my dirge
Through the heavy mist, the symbol of disdain emerges
Under this duress, I clash with a virge
In the uncanny night of this mundane world's purge.

The candlelight burned eternally,
And the sun glimmered like a quiet elegy.
I realize it's time to step out, jovially
To emphasize, not discount, the innocent silliness of loving, tirelessly.

The Adenium blooms where the path unfurls
For pride is the mask of our sins
The enlivening moon rises, leaving me asking
Will it shine over me or nestle its head on the clouds, masking?

Sweet nectar

Sweet nectar oh where are you
A little bird is looking for you
The need to quench her thirst and
Tiredness catching up to her again

Oh sweet nectar where are you
You are the only one who could
Relieve her of her ache
And turn her back into happy little
thing again

Oh sweet nectar where are you
Don't let her search go to vain

Compass

Your essence is a moonlit shore.
You move like the ocean—
An endless rhythm of calm and power
With eyes like lagoons where horizons meet.

The waves seem to sing your name
And as the ‘iwa takes flight to sing your glory
I’m led by Kaiona, to find your light
As you look like kindness and feel like home.

Where the kupuna and the keiki lay,
The sky carries constellations of us,
As they map a sky I’d spend forever learning
For you’re the compass I gravitate to.

Like sunsets painted in every hue.
You are the sanctuary of my soul’s restore.
If the ocean’s a mirror, it reflects only you,
An endless horizon, in infinite blue.

Pages of the heart

In the heart of the Rockies, where pine trees painted the horizon and the air was crisp with the scent of earth, Clara found herself at the crossroads of life. For years, she hustled in the suffocating confines of her corporate job, a whirl of spreadsheets and deadlines. Yet inside her, a different rhythm pulsed, one that danced to the beat of creativity, flavors, and the rustle of pages turning in a quiet bookshop.

The day she submitted her resignation felt surreal, like stepping off a cliff into an abyss filled with possibility. With her savings, she purchased a quaint cabin atop a secluded hill, its walls draped with ivy and its front porch offering a view of the valley below. Clara envisioned a bookstore café and inn, a refuge for tired souls seeking warmth and comfort among stories, where the aroma of freshly brewed coffee mingled with the musty sweetness of paper.

Months of hard work followed, but with each brick laid and every shelf filled, her dream began to take form. "The Nook" opened to the world, a whimsical hideaway where laughter echoed off wooden beams and patrons lost themselves in the pages of novels by the fire. Clara felt more alive than she ever had wearing a business suit.

Then came Eli, a wanderer with deep-set eyes and an enigmatic smile that hinted at stories untold. He stumbled upon The Nook one rainy afternoon, drenched but cheerful, as if the storm had chased him miles for this very purpose. Clara noticed his scars—not the kind etched on skin but those woven into his heart, dark shadows that fled beneath an easy laugh.

"Well, books and coffee on a rainy day. I think I've just stumbled upon heaven." He said giving a small chuckle.

Over cups of dark espresso and pastries that melted in the mouth, their connection blossomed. They shared dreams and fears, both hesitant yet yearning to expose their hearts completely. Clara was captivated by how Eli saw the beauty in the mundane; a cracked mug was a character study, and a sunset was an artwork vying for applause. But as the weeks passed, beneath Eli's charm lingered the weight of an unspoken burden, like a ghost that refused to part.

One evening, as the sun painted the sky in hues of orange and lavender, Eli broke the news that made Clara's heart loop into her stomach. He had to leave. A family emergency, he said, a call he couldn't ignore. "I'll be back," he promised, but his eyes betrayed him. He was a man who had mastered the art of saying goodbye.

The days turned into weeks, and Clara flipped through the pages of loneliness, the café echoing with the absence of laughter. Every sound reminded her of him—the creak of the floorboards, the gentle hiss of the espresso machine. She poured her heart into her work, but it felt insufficient, the café no longer a sanctuary but a reminder of what she had lost.

One rainy afternoon, as Clara closed up early, a familiar silhouette appeared at the door, silhouetted against the gray storm. Heart racing, she rushed to open it. Eli stood there, drenched again but this time buoyed by a smile that could melt the winter frost. "You didn't think I'd really leave you for good, did you?" he laughed, stepping inside.

Clara's heart soared as she embraced him, their warmth filling the air. He explained how he had traveled back as quickly as he could, drawn by a fierce realization that he couldn't live without her or the world they began creating together.

"I thought my past would always anchor me, but I realized it only made me appreciate the freedom of the present more," Eli confessed, his fingers entwining with hers as they huddled in front of the fire.

"I found a new path. I want to be with you, to build our lives here together."

Tears filled Clara's eyes, not of sorrow but of joy. Against the backdrop of their shared dreams, they felt the weight of their pasts begin to dissolve, replaced by promises of tomorrow.

Together they navigated the challenges of love, healing each other through shared laughter and quiet moments. Clara's bookstore café and inn flourished, and so did their bond, entwining stories of resilience and grace. In the heart of the mountains, amidst the rustle of pages and the aroma of coffee, Clara and Eli found a home, not just in The Nook but within each other's hearts.

And sometimes, in the corners of that cozy café, you could hear whispers of love with every turn of a page, with every new dawn that promised another beautiful chapter in their lives.

The Two of Us

(translation of 'Ormakal' by Akash Roopesh from Malayalam to English by Athulya M.)

The hour had ventured beyond dawn's embrace. The sky up above that makes the river flow wept fervently. Just as always, I cocooned in my blankets, enjoying the gentle chill of the rain. In the stillness of the moment, I felt a gradual presence- as though someone was sitting next to me.

"Time to wake up, son. It has been a while". It was my father.

Failing to heed his words, I slowly slipped into an easeful slumber like how the clouds nestle against the moon. He nudged me again, to draw my focus.

"Just need some more time..." Saying so, I descended again to sleep. In the midst of it, I was conscious of my father telling me, "I'm leaving" after placing his gentle kiss on my forehead. Time was marching forward.

When the clock struck past teI stormed to the kitchen only to see my mother standing on the counter shocked, with tears welling up in her eyes. Slowly, she lifted her face to meet my gaze. Without uttering another word, I quietly walked out of the kitchen.

The relentless torrents of the somber clouds continued to fall from heaven's grace. The winds unleashed their mighty howls. The trees and shrubs were swaying to the wind, just like my tormenting mind.

n, I slowly arose from my tranquil sleep. Upon leaving my room, I yelled out for my mother to which she responded, "Ah, you're up! Go on brush your teeth, it's been a while, hasn't it?" Tuning out her words, I asked her louder this time, "When did Dad go?" Silence hung in the air.

It's been two years since the passing of my father. The weight of time feels like all of it was yesterday. I still can't believe it. Just like every other day, I bid adieu to my father before leaving. Had I known that was the last day I'd ever see him, I would've looked at him a little longer. To embrace that familiar warmth and comfort that reflected from his face.

As I kept walking outside, I stared vividly at the blank, overcast sky. The raindrops kept falling on my face transporting me to those precious bygone days. And there, on the other side of silence, I met my father.

He was returning home in his same, old bike. It was a heavy downpour even there. "Hold your father tightly". Hearing that, I clung to him with determination, leaning against him. Despite the deluge, that little boy was fearless because his father's warmth and comfort amidst the tempest kept him brave. The spirit of the little boy warmed. He smiled peacefully.

Those memories were fading quickly. In that rain, I wailed with deep pain. I surrendered to the deep sea of pain, loss, and agony, leaving me alone and adrift in the sea of profound sorrow and melancholy. Suddenly, I felt a hand, a familiar gentle touch, on my shoulder.

"Son".

I turned back only to see my father behind me.

"Father."

My eyes glimmered.

"Why are you crying, my dear?", my father asked me.

"How could you leave without telling me anything? How can you not acknowledge my presence and pass me by?"

He chuckled lightly. "Oh son, were you crying because you were thinking about me? All my life, I worked hard for you, to see you happy and now you weep thinking of me?"

"But... you're no longer here with me to share my joys with me. Why did you leave fast?"

"Why did I leave? I did not want this too, my beloved son but time took me away from the path I wanted to live in. I was trying to tell you of this farewell. I just wasn't able to."

I fixed my gaze on him and wiped my tears.

"Then who told you I'm not with you?", asked my father. "I can never leave you. I will always live in the little sanctuary of your mind, only to celebrate every joys and sorrows with you, son. Do not ever grieve thinking about me. You are never alone. There are so many people beside you who love you dearly. Keep them close."

I hugged my father tightly. To feel his warmth just like the gentle sunshine.

"But father, it is these very memories that make me sad."

"Memories are beautiful, dear son. There will be memories that will never fade. Cherish and protect them. Sometimes, those memories will be disheartening but without memories or experiences, what meaning and purpose does life have, isn't it? There's beauty in anything when you move ahead with memories and it's lessons. People you have loved deeply can also become memories but you need to push forward happily and courageously. Own your memories. For, it is with the demise of your memories you cease to exist too."

"Father, I love you more than this entire world", I told him.
"I'm aware. I know it, my boy". My father placed a tender, gentle kiss on my forehead. It had everything in it.
He looked at me and smiled again. I knew it was his time to say goodbye. That was his acknowledgment.
In that very rain, my father quietly slipped away leaving behind the cherished memories and fond moments that came rushing into my mind like the downpour that night. I basked in the glory of that moment with my eyes closed. It continued to rain heavily. Traversing through those memories, I felt a smile across my face. The same smile that I experienced, epochs ago.

Author's bio

Anvitha Hegde is a poet and an avid reader based in Bengaluru. She enjoys poetry and fiction and has an immense passion for reading and writing. She is a Throwball player, who loves all things cozy. She is currently pursuing her undergarduate degree majoring in English Literature in Kristu Jayanti College in Bengaluru.

Hailing from Kerala, Athulya M. Anilkumar, an undergraduate student at Kristu Jayanti College, majors in English language and literature. She is involved in poetry, research, and story-telling. In her free time, she enjoys astronomy, natural sciences, origami, and photography.

www.ingramcontent.com/pod-product-compliance
Lightning Source LLC
LaVergne TN
LVHW041257150826
845673LV00008B/2630

* 9 7 9 8 8 9 6 9 9 8 9 1 4 *